The 'Mary Had a Little Lamb' Book

for Violin

by Cassia Harvey

CHP168
©2014 by C. Harvey Publications All Rights Reserved.
www.charveypublications.com - print books & free sheet music blog
www.learnstrings.com - PDF downloadable books & chamber music

1. Mary Had a Little Lamb

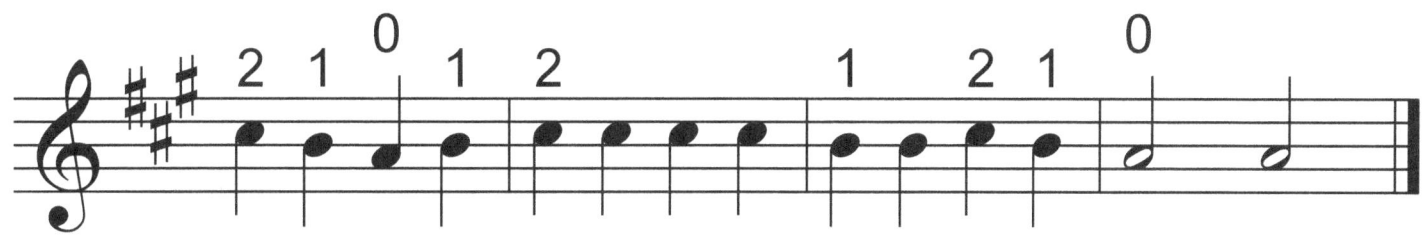

2. Mary Had Some Whole Notes

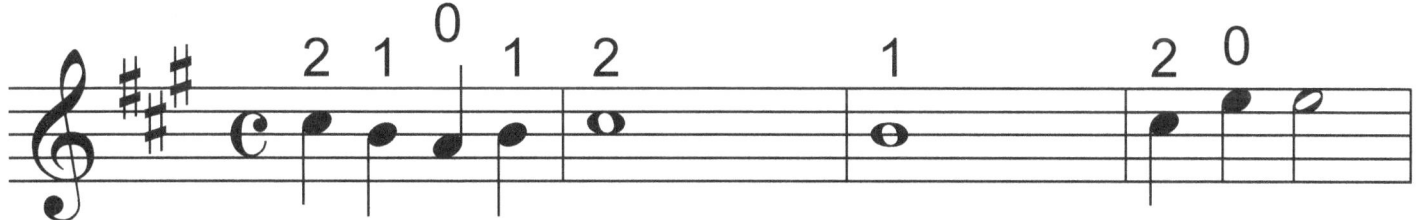

3. Mary Runs After the Lamb

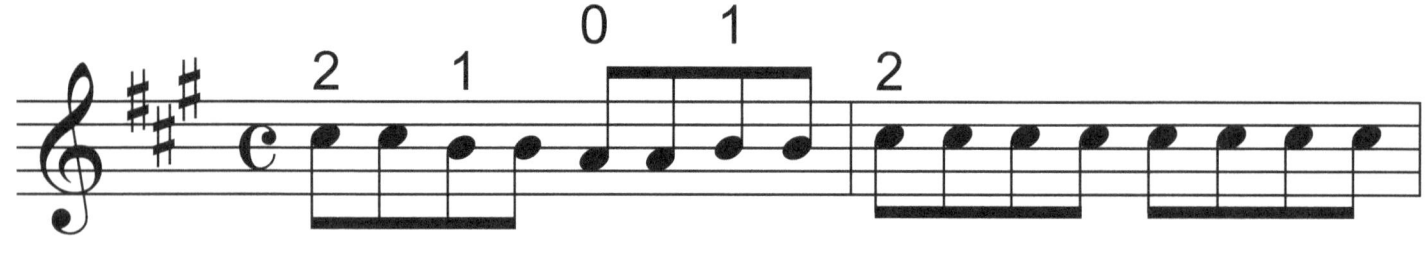

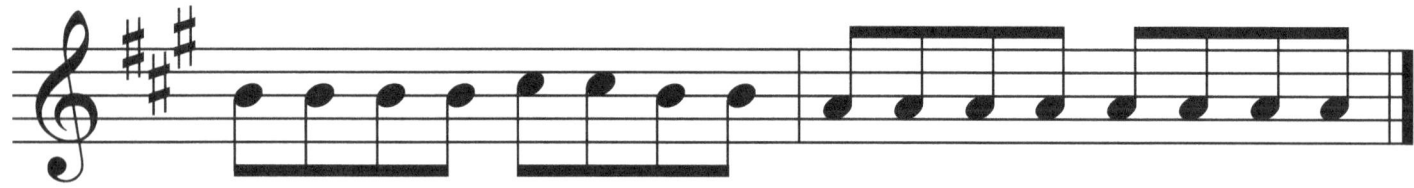

4. Mary's Rhythm

5. Running and Crossing Strings

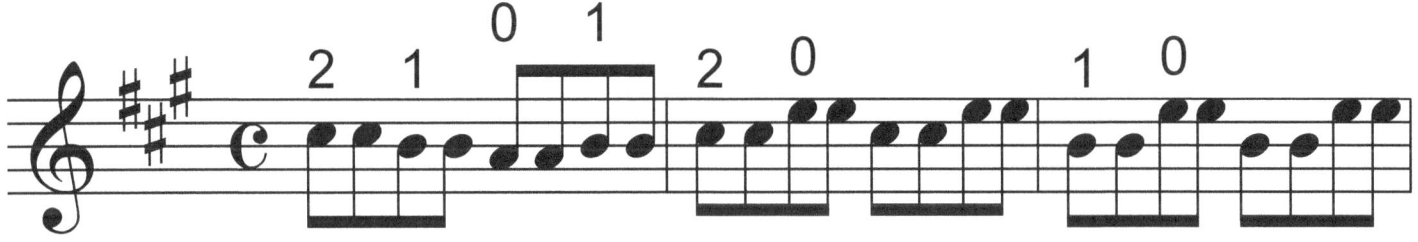
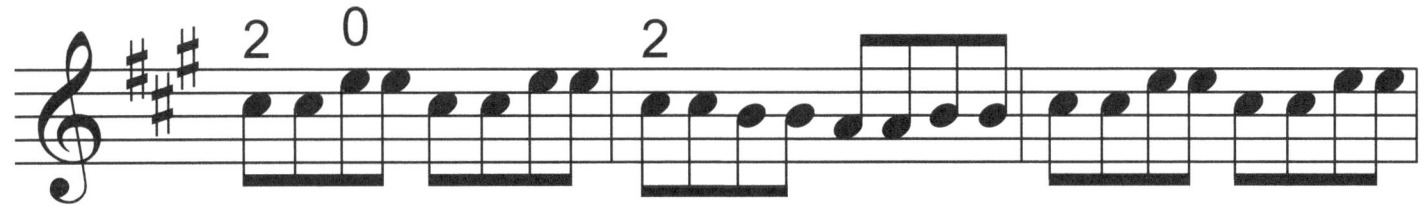

6. Mary Had a Little Lamb on E

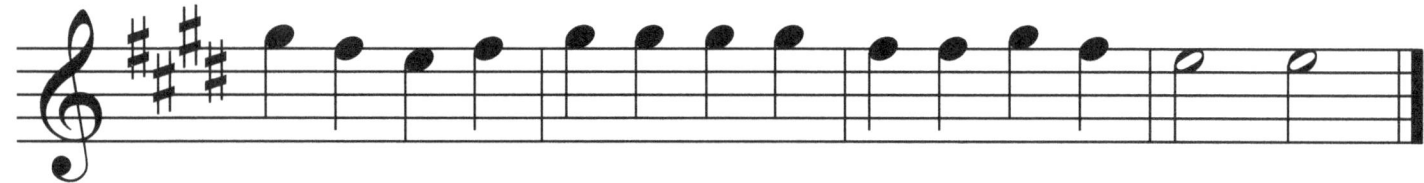

7. Lamb's Rhythm

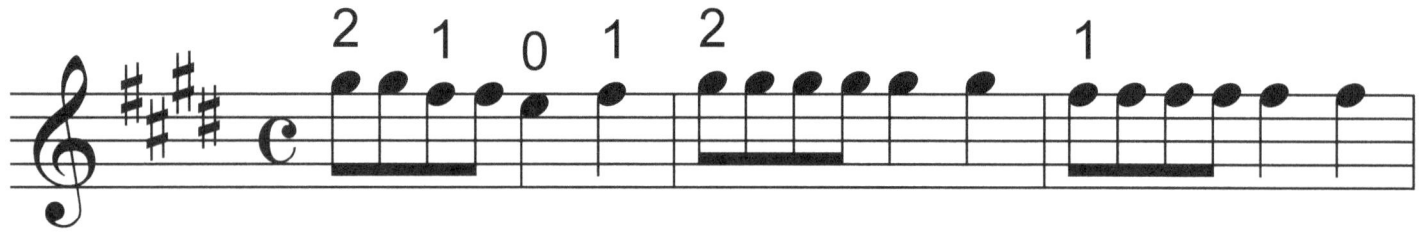
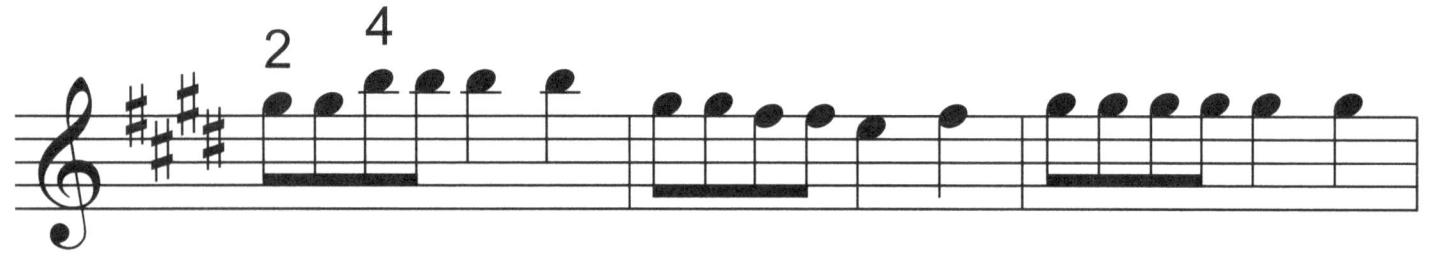

8. Mary is Marching

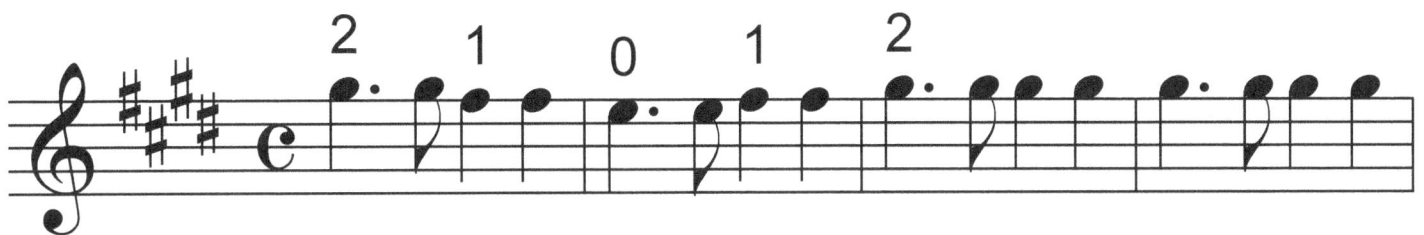
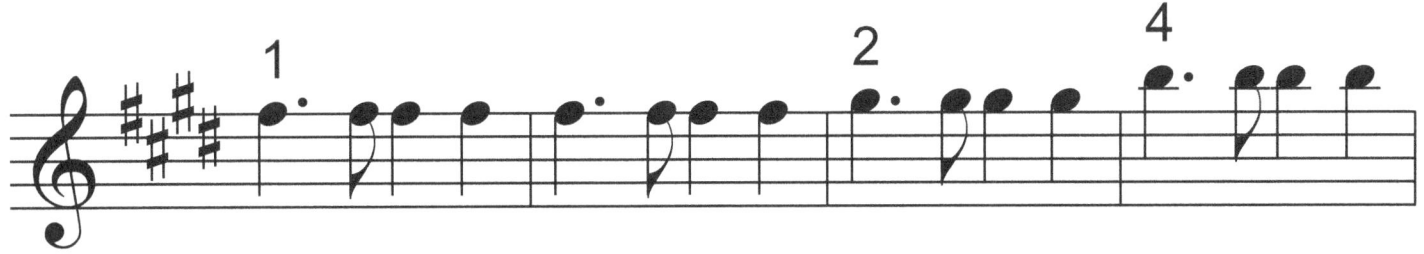

9. Playing Slurs with Mary

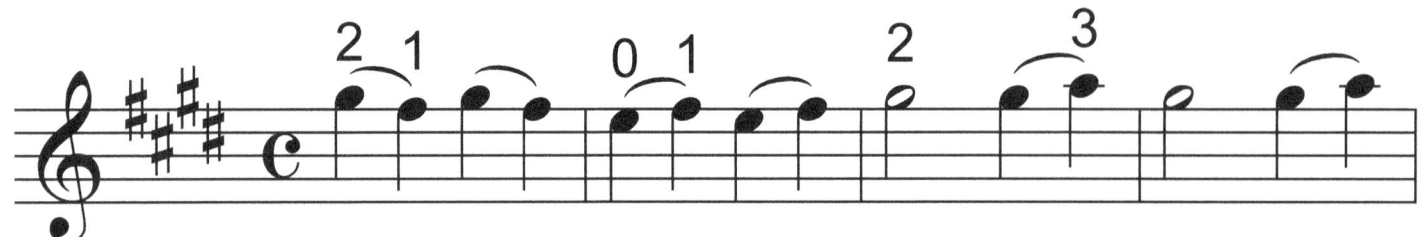

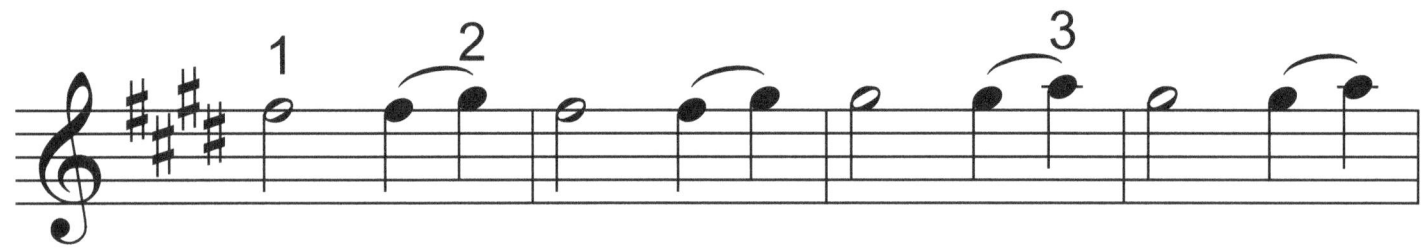

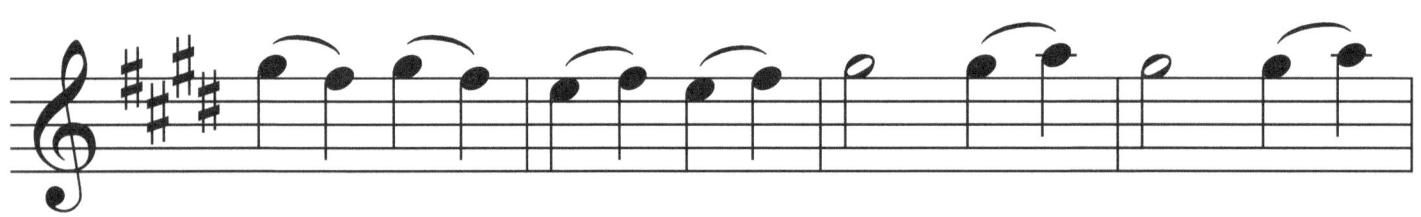

10. Mary Had a Little Lamb on D

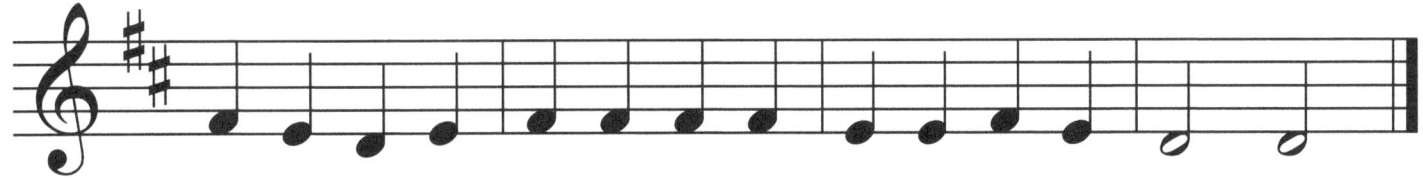

11. Lamb Rhythm

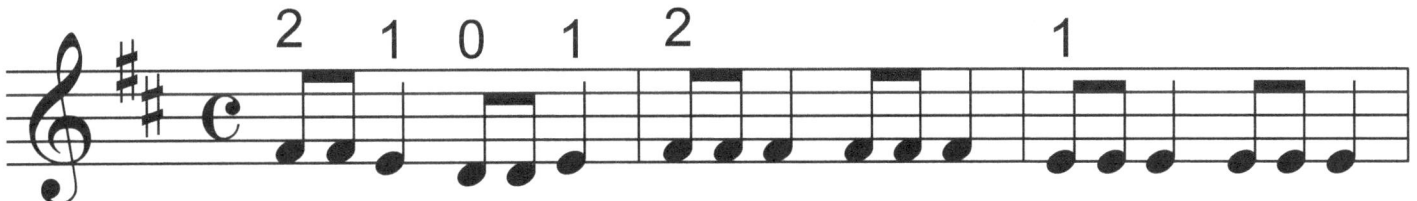

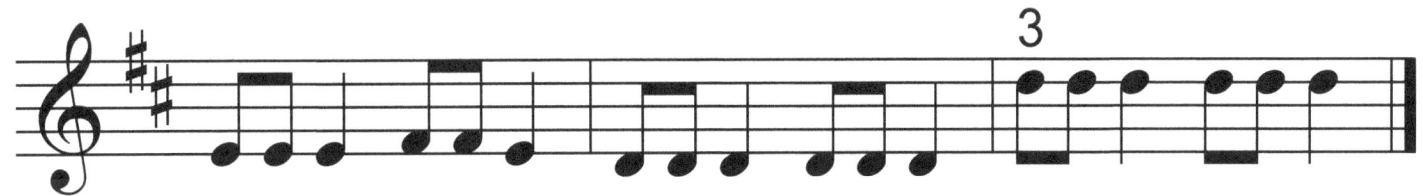

12. Mary's String Changing

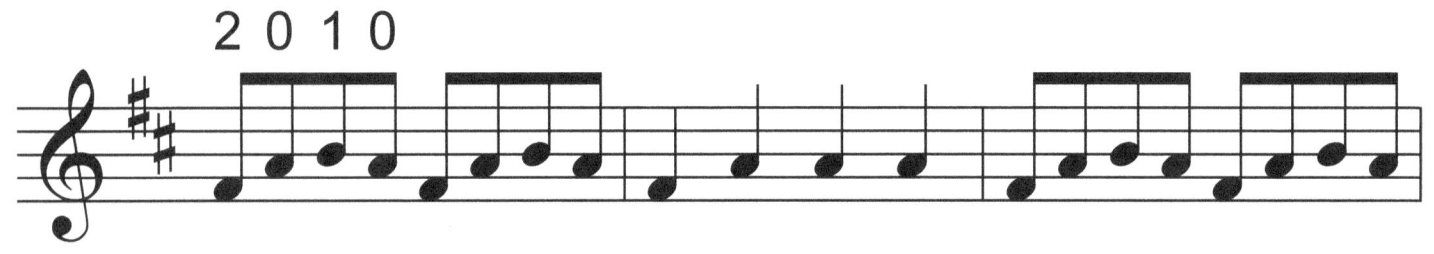
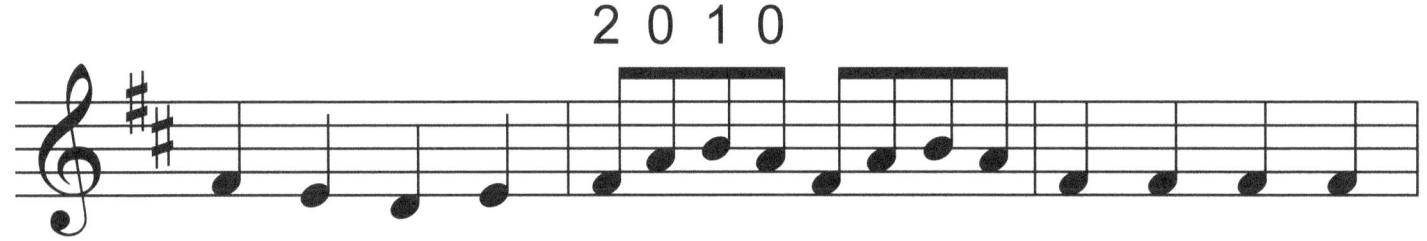
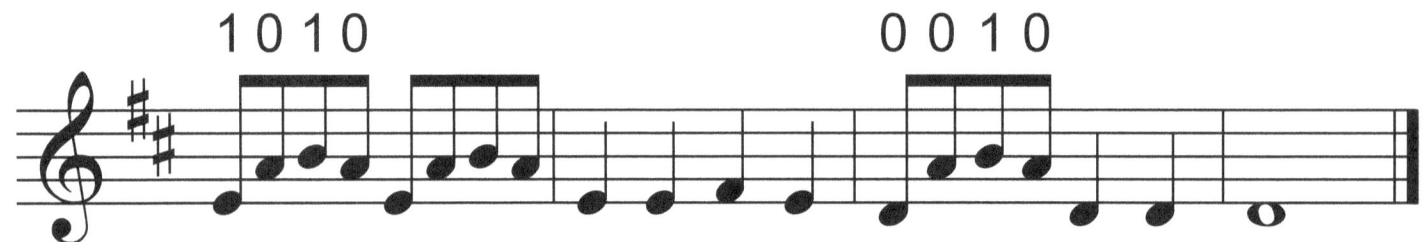

13. Mary's Finger Exercise

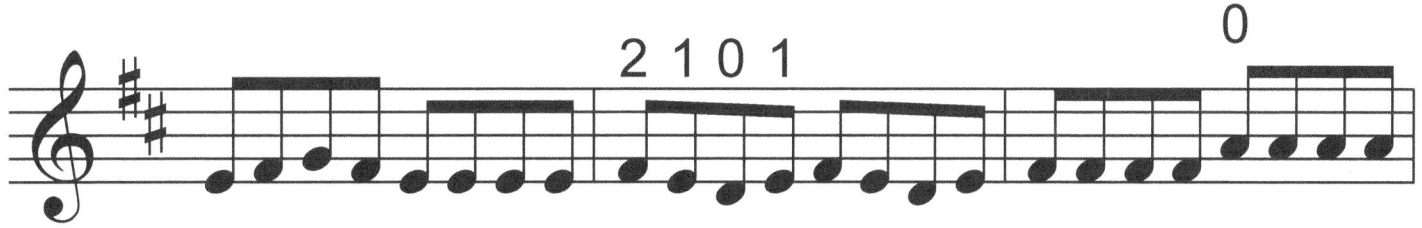

14. Mary Had a Little Lamb on G

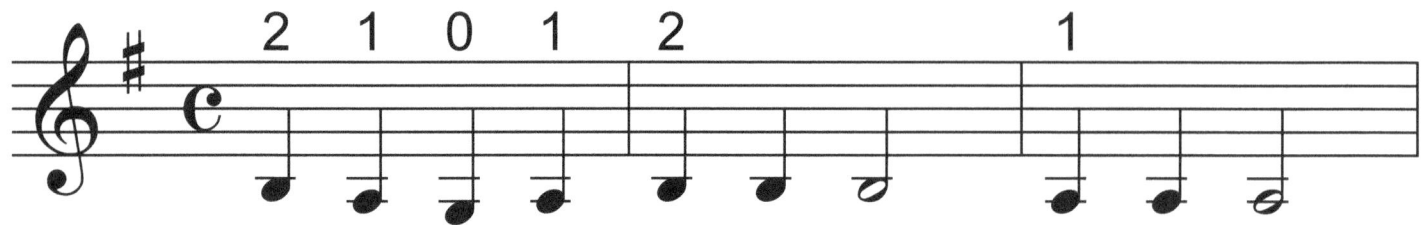
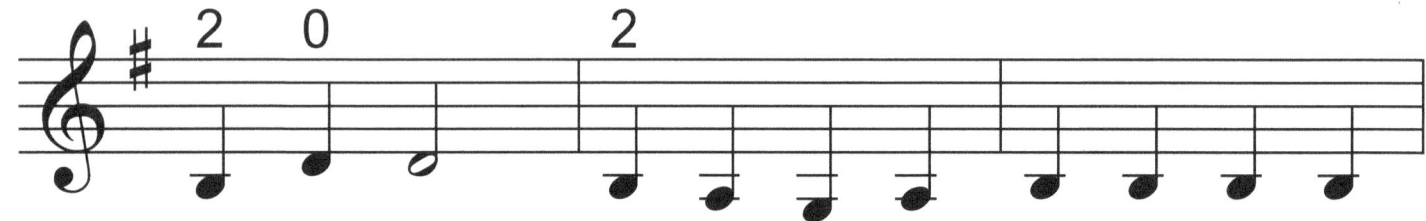

15. Lamb With Dotted Half Notes

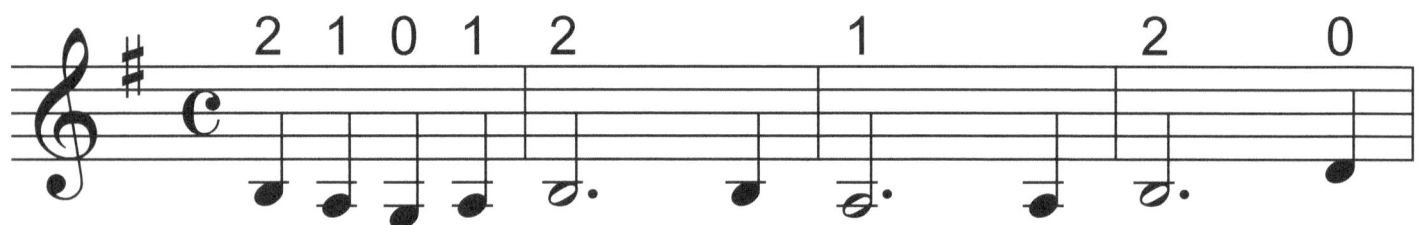
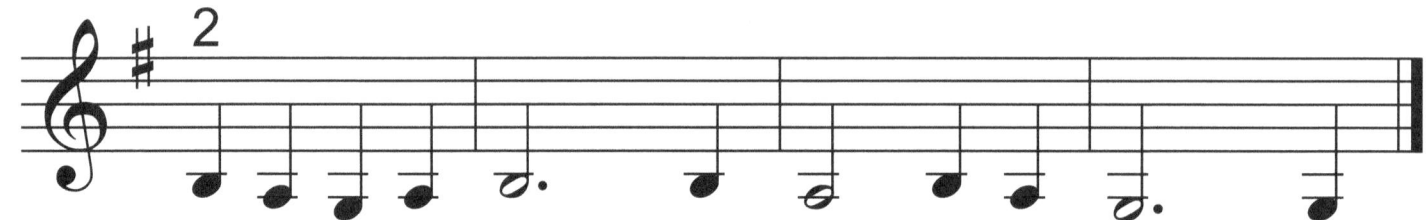

16. Mary's Rhythm

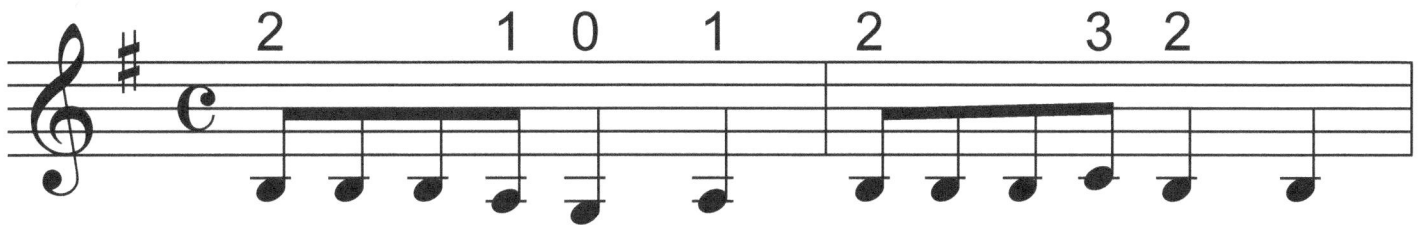
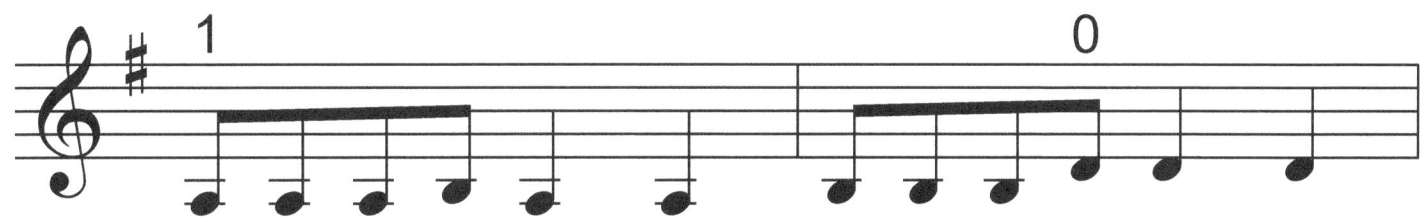
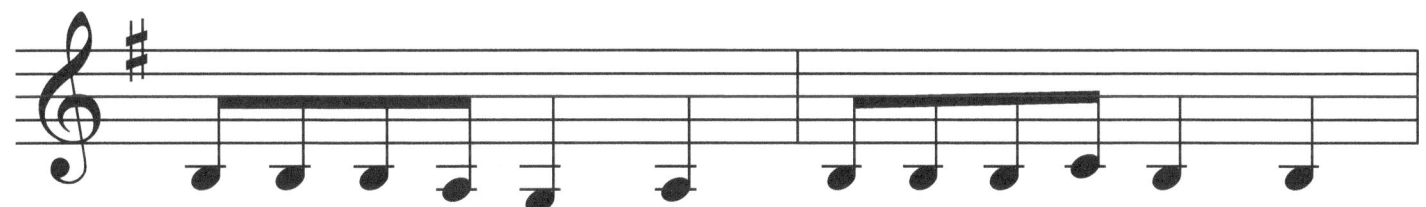
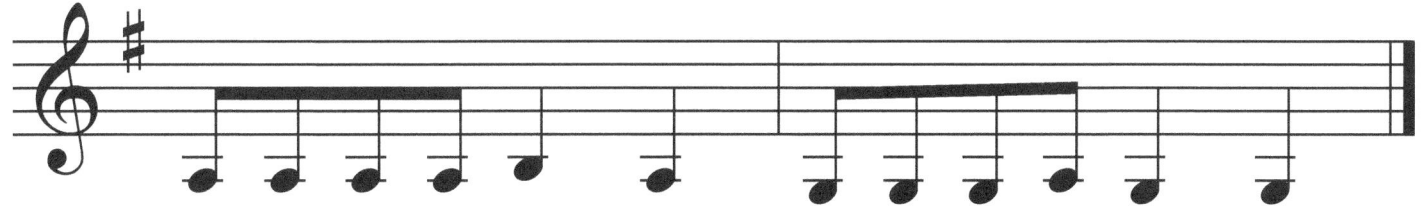

17. Mary Changes Strings

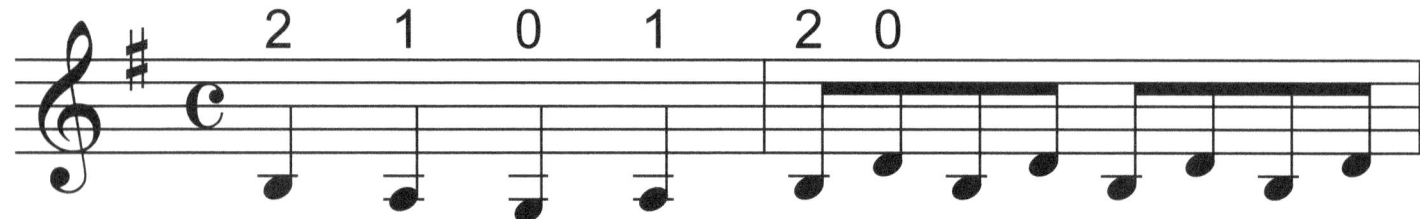
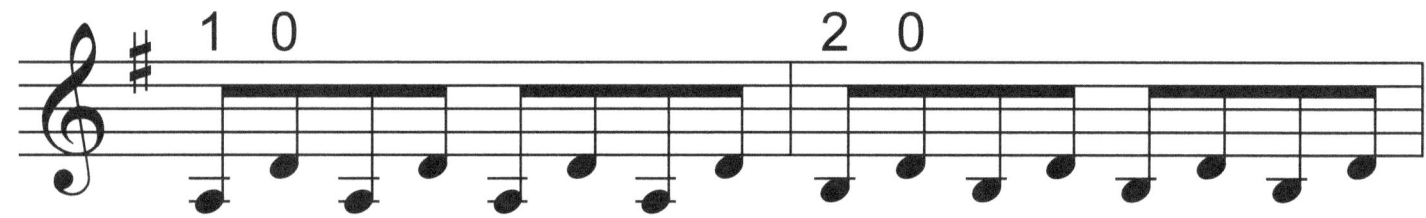
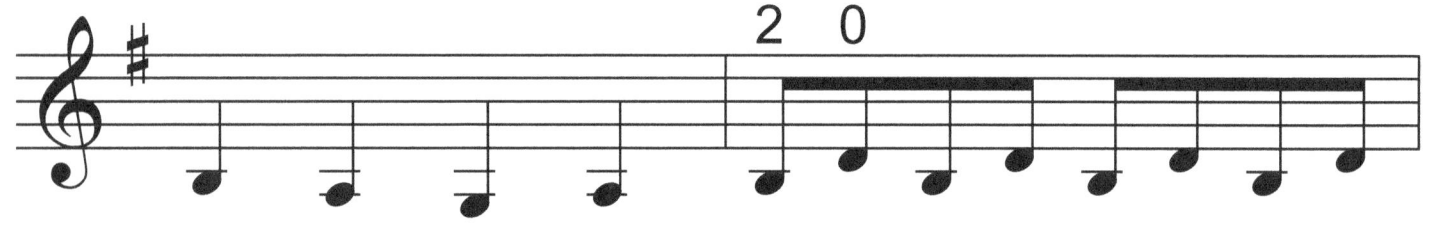
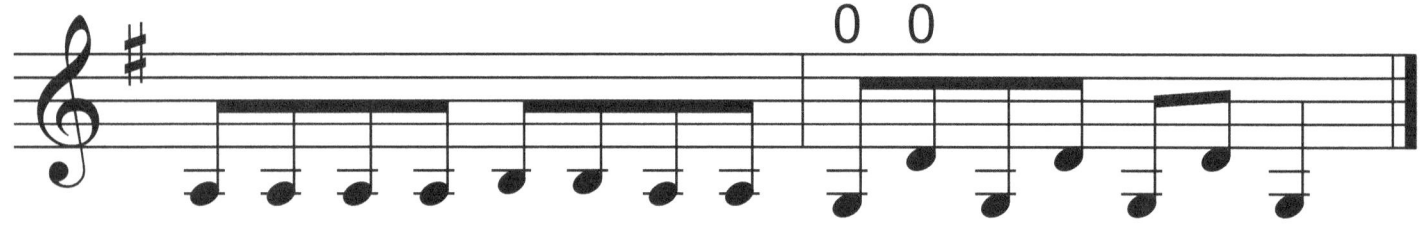

18. Mary Lost Her Little Lamb

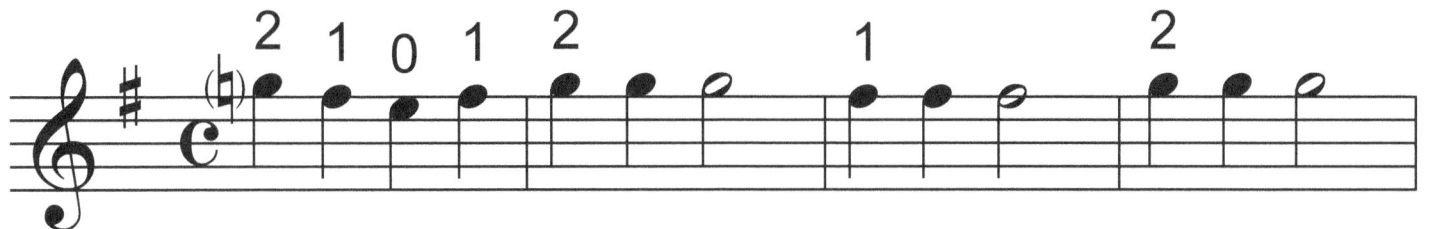

19. Lost Lamb Slurs

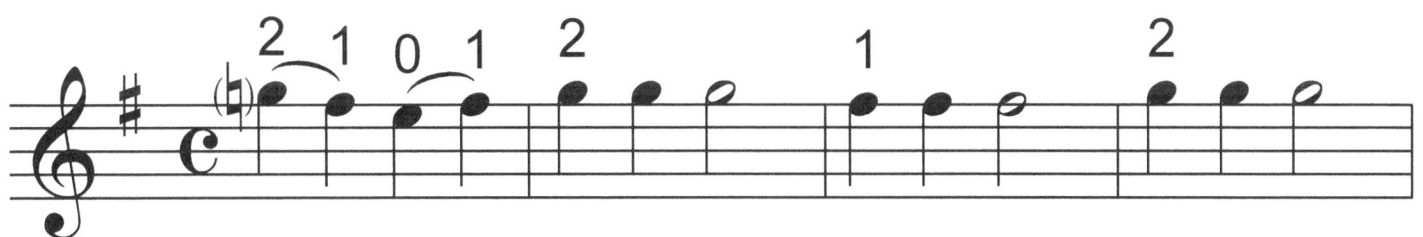
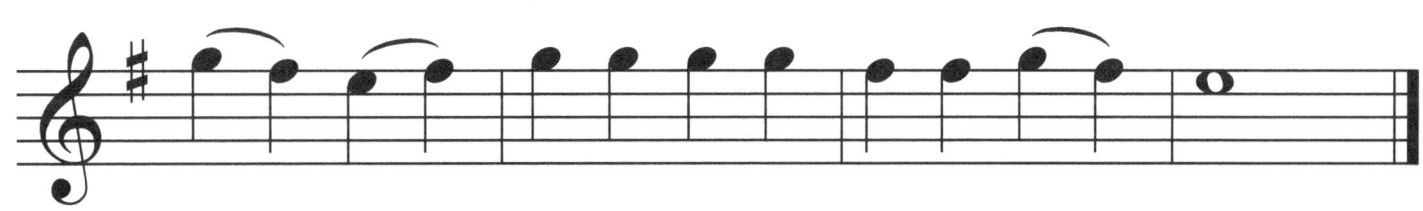

20. Mary Lost Her Little Lamb on A

21. Lost Lamb in 3/4

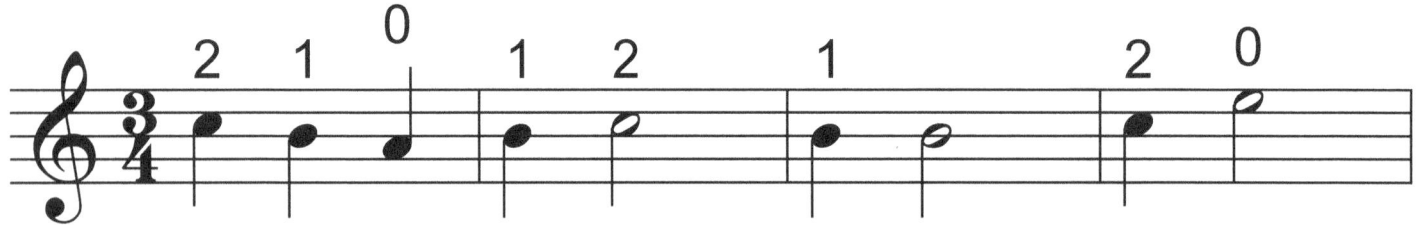

22. Mary Lost Her Little Lamb on D

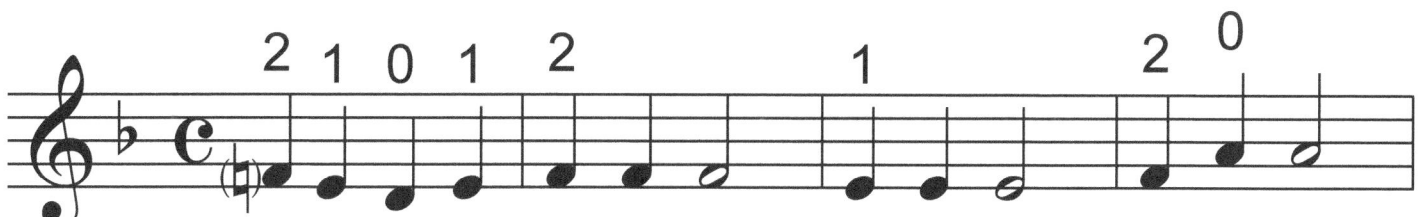

23. Lost Lamb in 6/8

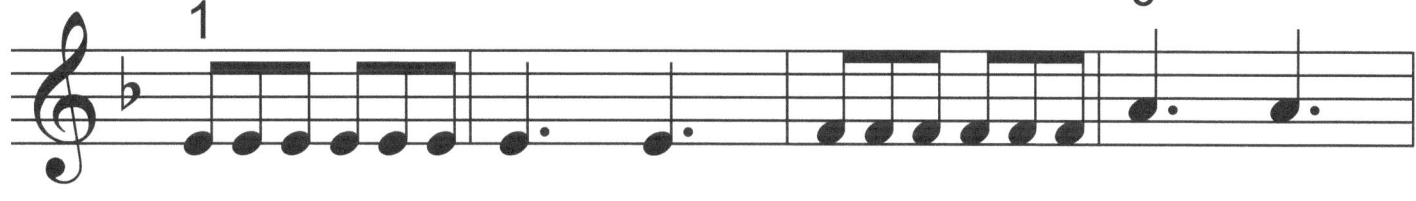

24. Mary Lost Her Little Lamb on G

25. Lost Lamb in 2/4

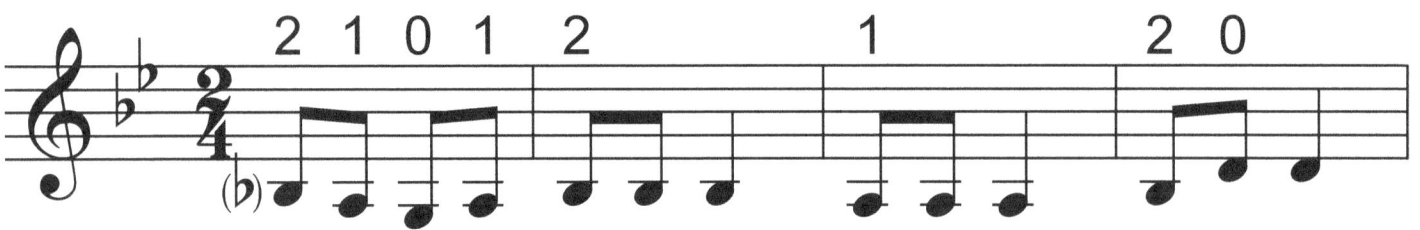

26. Mary Starts on First Finger

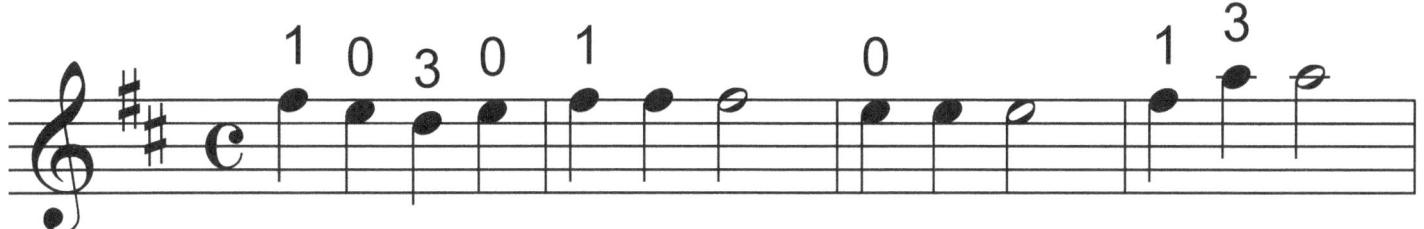
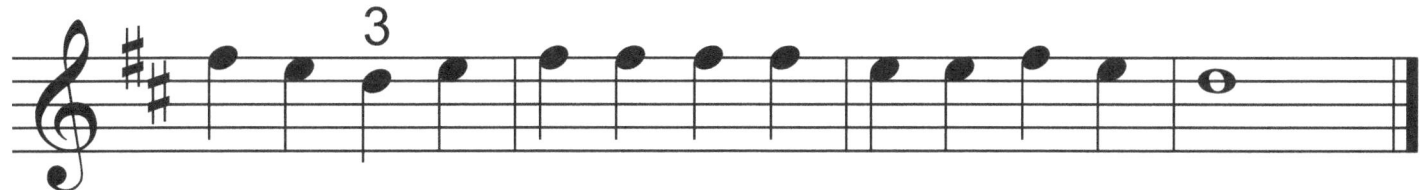

27. Lamb Slurs

28. Mary's 6/8 Counting

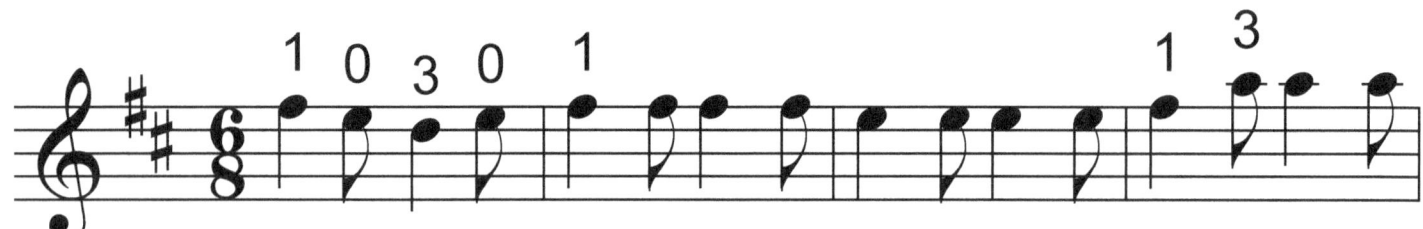

29. Lamb Stops

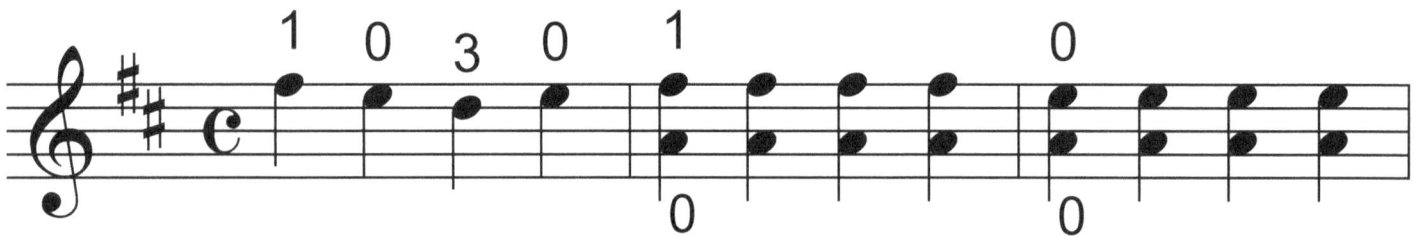

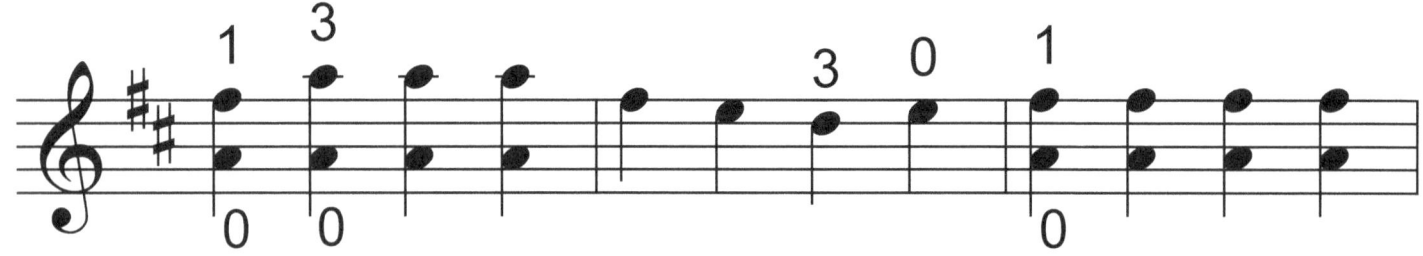

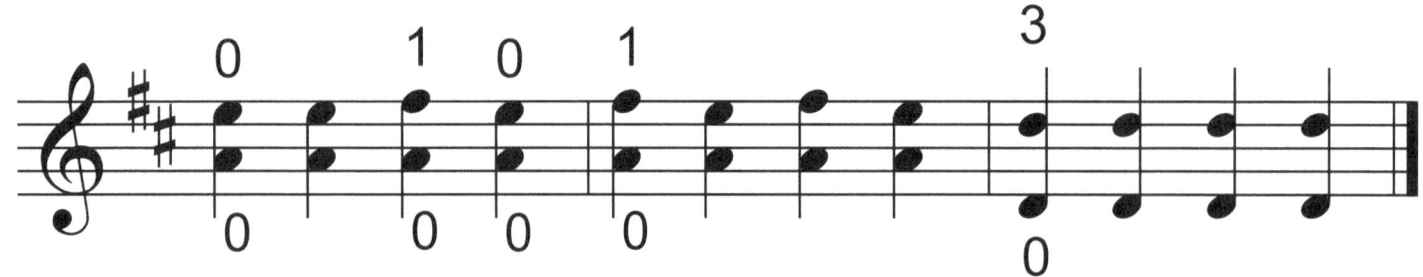

30. Mary Starts on First Finger

31. Mary's Rhythm

32. Lamb Slurs

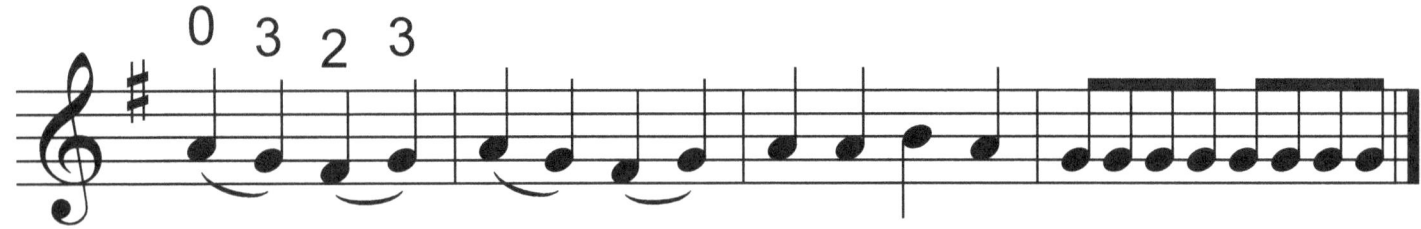

33. Mary Starts on First Finger

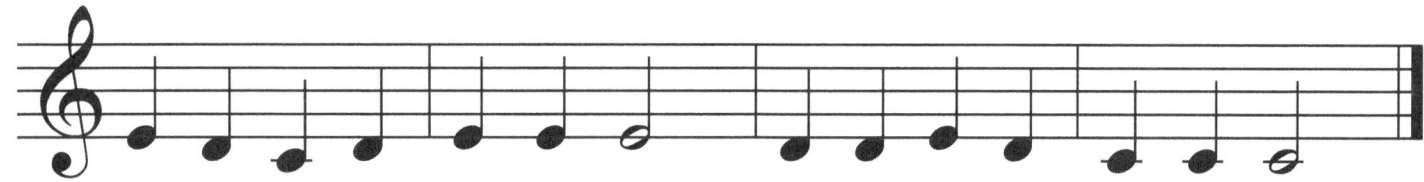

34. Lamb Dance in 6/8

35. Mary's Slurs

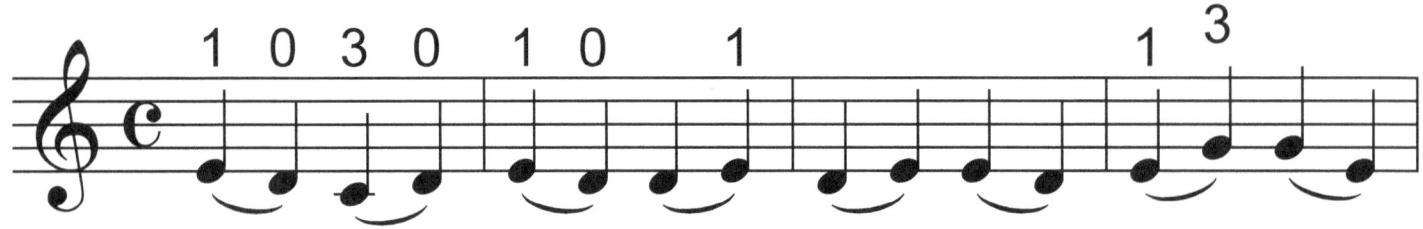

36. Mary Goes Running

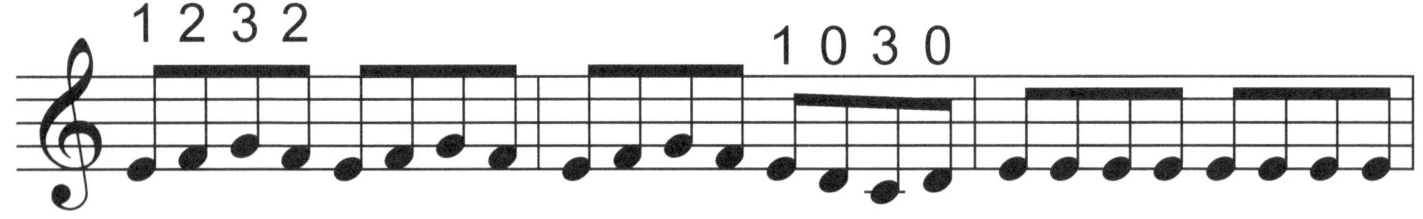
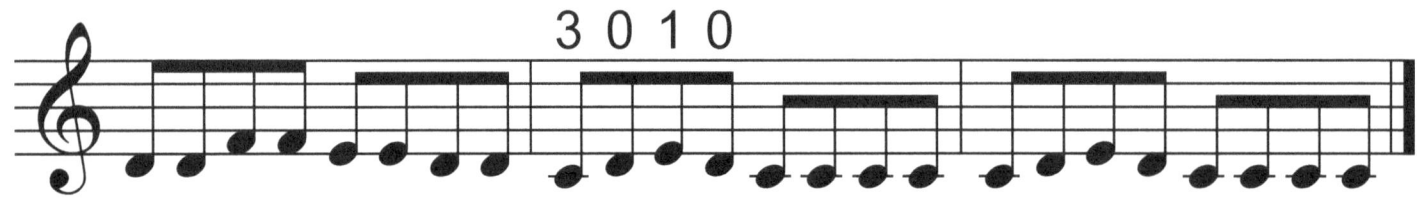

37. Mary Starts on Open E

38. Lamb Crossing

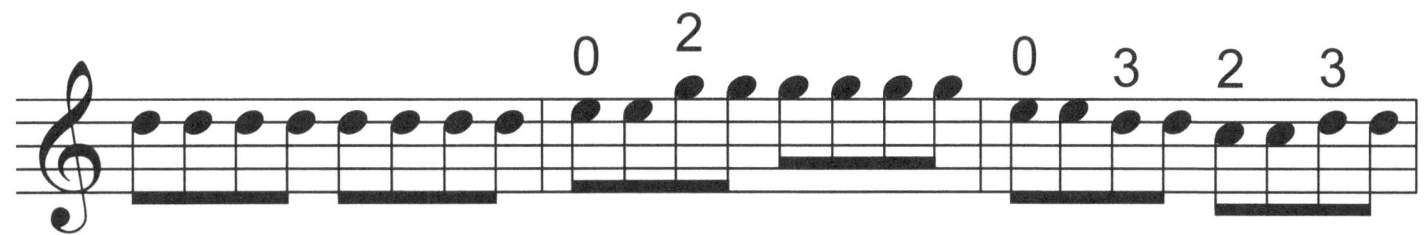
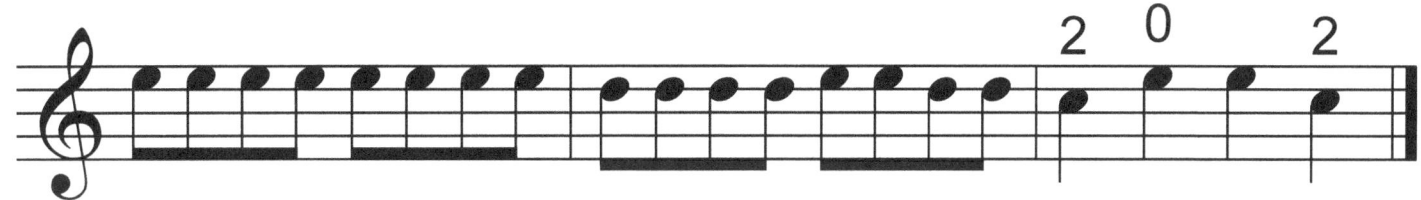

39. Mary's Rhythm

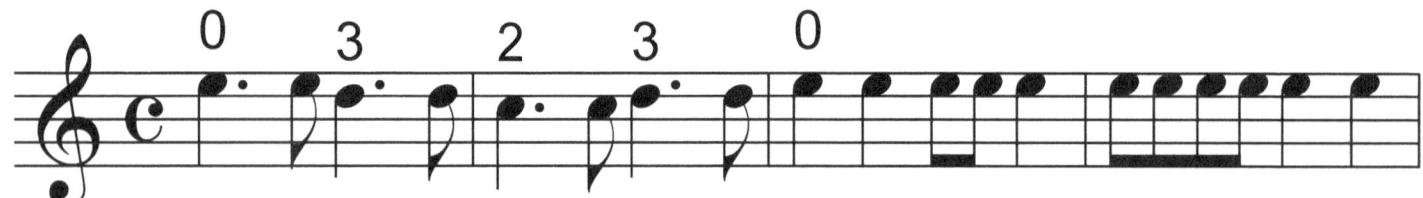
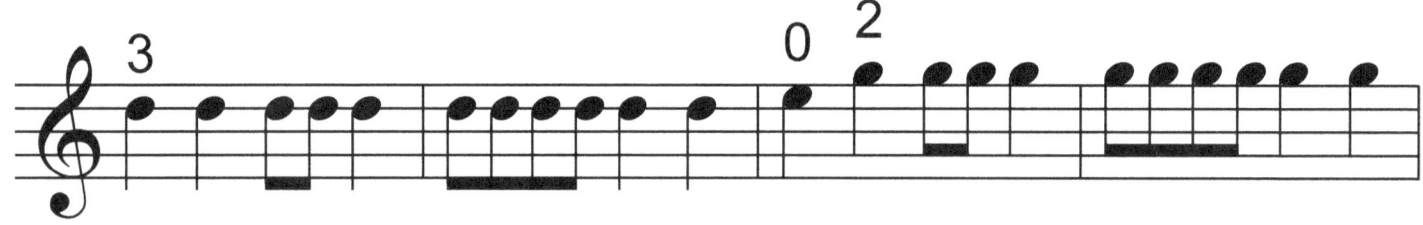

40. Mary Starts on Open A

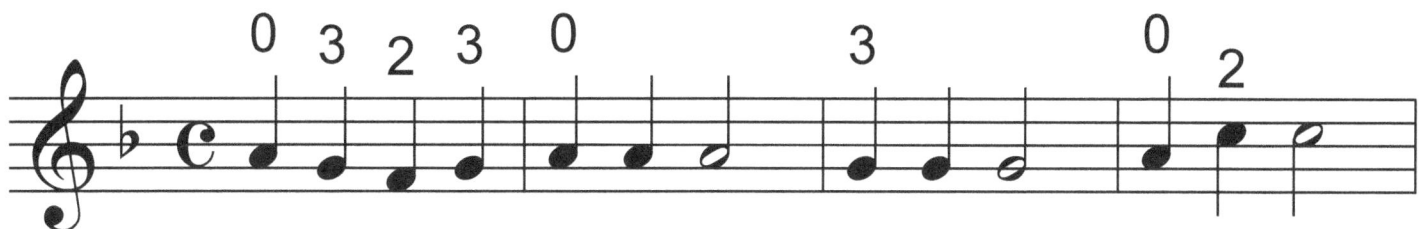

41. Mary's Dotted Quarter Notes

42. Mary in 3/4

43. Lamb Stops

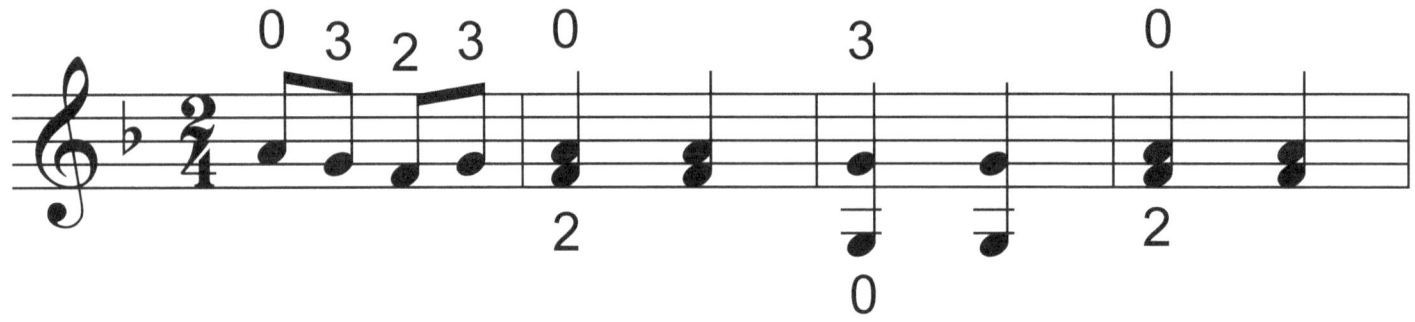
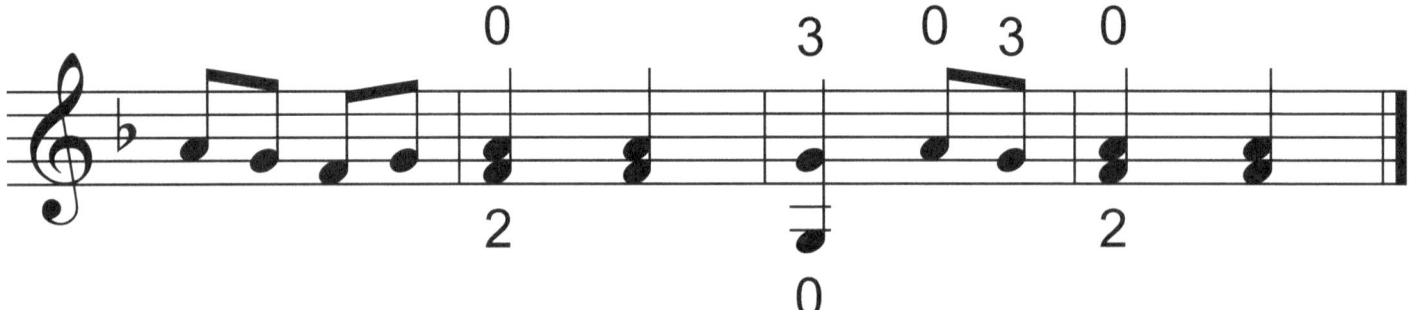

44. Mary Starts on Open D

45. Lamb in 3/4

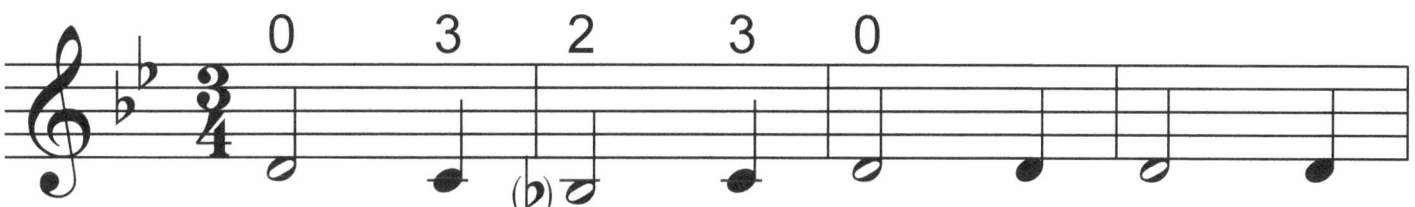
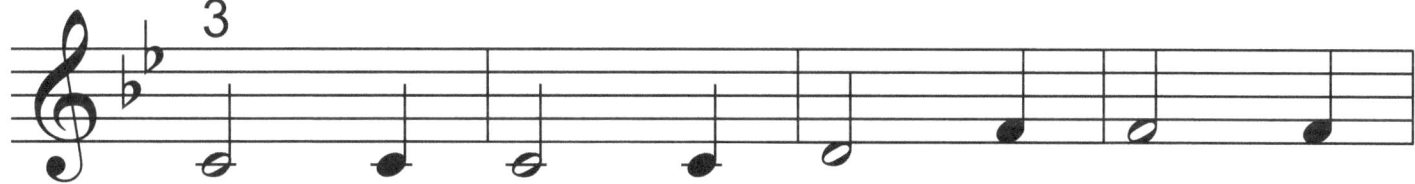
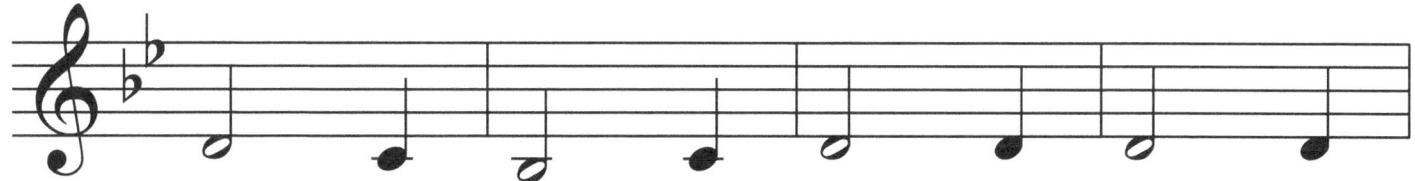
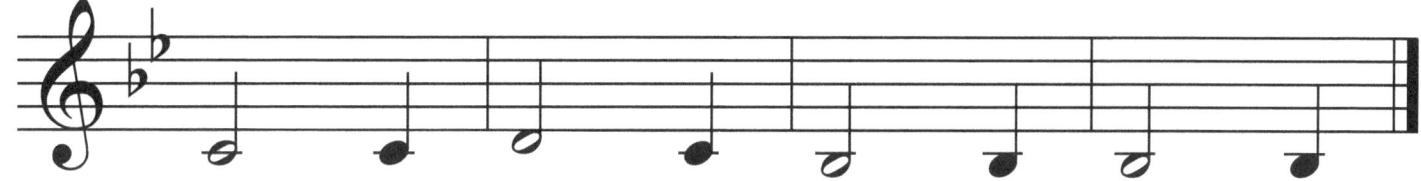

46. Mary Rests

47. Lamb Octaves

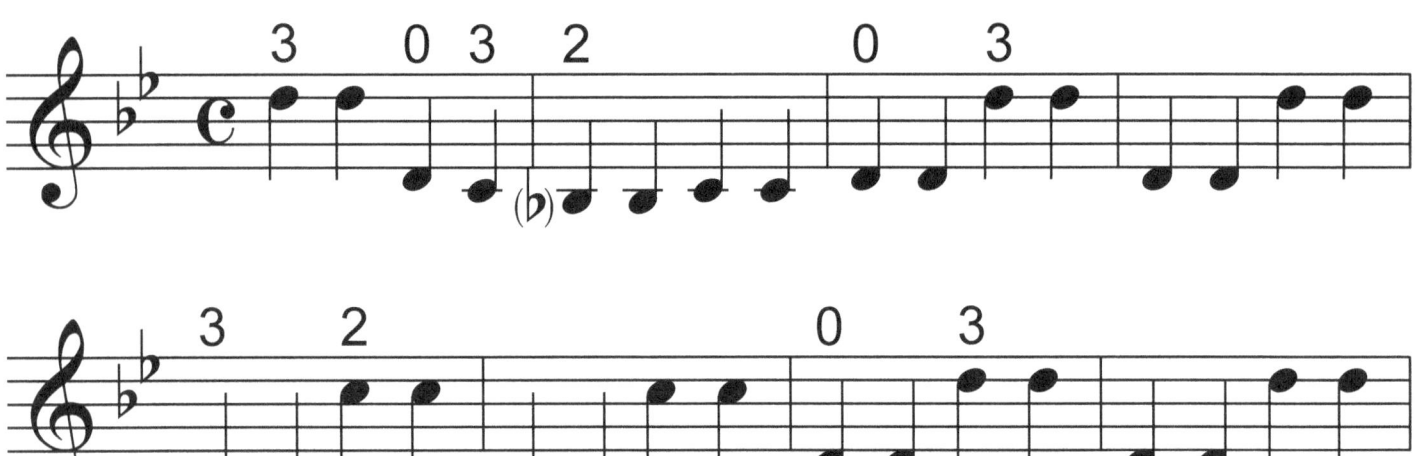

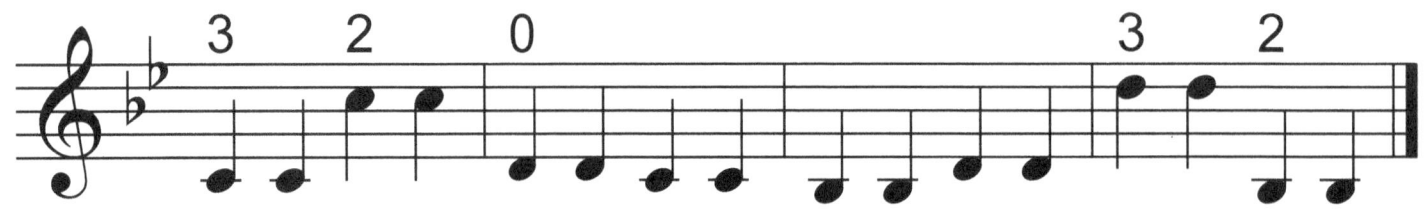

48. Lamb Bowing

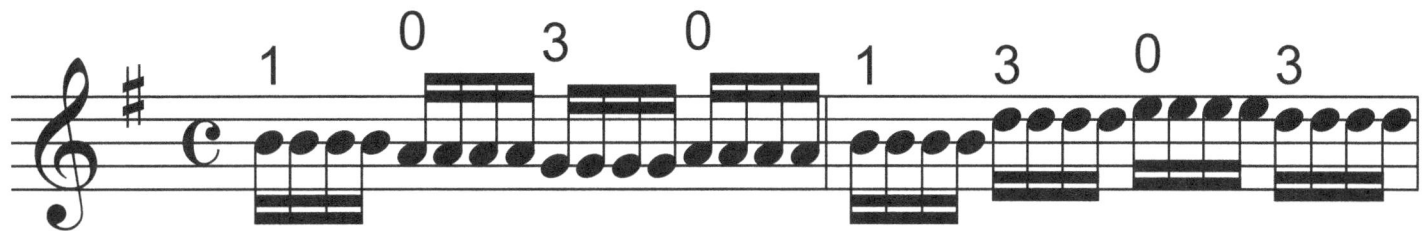
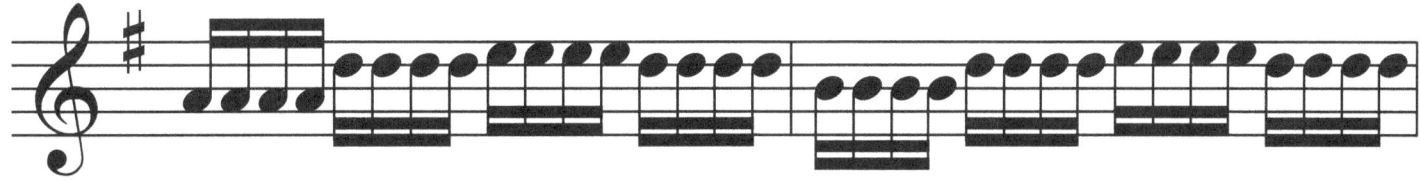

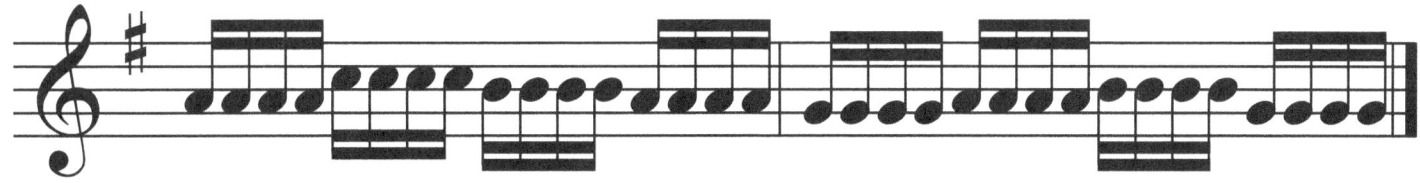

49. Mary's Fiddle Tune

50. The Lamb's Fiddle Tune

available from **www.charveypublications.com**: CHP303

Beginning Fiddle Duets for Two Violins

Cripple Creek

Trad., arr. Myanna Harvey

©2016 C. Harvey Publications All Rights Reserved.

www.ingramcontent.com/pod-product-compliance
Lightning Source LLC
Chambersburg PA
CBHW081130080526
44587CB00021B/3818